SURVIVAL FOOD TO STOCKPILE

With a comprehensive list of essentials, you and your family can survive any disaster in the comfort of your own home.

William Brown

Copyright © 2022 by William Brown All rights reserved.

No portion of this book may be reproduced in any form without written permission from the publisher or author, except as permitted by U.S. copyright law.

Contents

1. INTRODUCTION   1
2. ESSENTIAL FOODS TO STOCK   14
3. Several Instruments for Making and Fixing Things   35
4. BEGIN RIGHT NOW TO COMPILE YOUR FOOD STASH FROM SCRATCH   81
5. HOW TO EFFICIENTLY MANAGE YOUR FOOD SUPPLIES.   103
6. lists twelve different methods for keeping food fresh.   126

Chapter 1

INTRODUCTION

On that recent Sunday afternoon in the winter, my sister-in-law Rachel could not have anticipated that in a few hours, she would be stranded in the snow for more than two weeks without enough food.

In 2015, the authorities warned that an abnormally huge snowstorm will affect a large portion of our nation.

As he continued to paint his replica of a Ferrari Testarossa from the 1990s, her husband shrugged. "Calm down, you're putting too much stock in the news."

She offers him a nod as she passes him to retrieve the pickup's keys before rushing out to the grocery store.

She comes to a stop in the doorway, looks up, and freezes for a moment in disbelief.

The houses are engulfed in a dark mass of the sky that is in the distance. You could almost reach up and touch the clouds, so real they seem.

And if we were trapped inside, what would we do for food? she thought.

She rushes to the first store after hopping in the truck and firing up the engine as soon as she could, as if she had to flee an attack. However, as she turns onto the main street, she is forced to brake hard to prevent a rear-end collision.

The same direction is being driven by a line of cars. She said to herself, "Shit, this really is an emergency." She manages to be to the shopping center in under an hour thanks to the fact that the supermarket is typically only 10 minutes away and the traffic.

During rush hour, the typically vacant parking lot resembles an international airport.

Arrivals, departures, and disagreements over parking spots are all common occurrences.

Horns, taunts, and general anxiety all but persuade her to turn around and head back home. She steels herself, telling herself, "NO, I have a family to feed, and food supplies are the top concern." You must enter that food store regardless of the circumstances!

She notices a free parking lot out of the corner of her eye. She does it with her and only her without disagreeing with anyone as she accelerates just enough. It's almost there. In the midst of the crowd, she leaps from the car.

Rachel succeeds in entering amidst pushing and arguments over the age-old "I was there first" controversy.

Everyone is speaking at once, which is chaotic and loud. The now-"looted" alleys were filled with people roaming aimlessly.

The refrigerators' doors are open but empty.

The quickest, sturdiest individuals carrying overflowing trolleys to the register.

Theft of food from neighboring carts is also occurring.

A greedy and out-of-control throng storms the employee who is trying to replenish the shelves.

A fistfight is developing.

Why is my hubby absent whenever I need him?

The lines at the cash register are lengthy and tense, with each person jealously eyeing the items in the other's cart and guarding their own.

Rachel experiences a lump in her throat and escalating panic that causes her to gasp for air.

"I'll have to go, it's awful, they're crazy," she exclaimed.

She pushes her way past the crowd to the car and then into her house.

Even worse than on the drive there, there is more traffic.

There is a general panic taking hold, as evidenced by the lines at gas stations.

When Rachel arrives home, she gives the dark sky behind her one more glance before going inside.

"I returned without any gifts. It had no chance. We will just need to pray.

She slams the door, dumps her luggage on the ground, and starts to take heavy steps in the direction of her husband, who is still with his blasted models.

He can only turn to face her and be ashamed and embarrassed that he did nothing.

All he can hear her saying is, "I told you..., I warned you.," whether she says it out or not.

But he now realizes that the only thing they can do is wait while praying for the best.

***

Exactly why did I tell you this tale?

I do this because I want you to understand that anything can happen at any time, even something unexpected.

There are numerous problems that our civilization must deal with, including wars, pandemics, climate change, the rapid growth of the world's population, the degradation of forests, and the ongoing extinction of animal and plant species.

However, even the news of an excessive snowstorm can send people into a panic before they consider the devastating changes that could bring about the dissolution of our civilization.

In fact, at the first symptoms of a world crisis or a natural disaster, consumers have frequently in recent years quickly vacated stores.

A good example of this is in 2015, when the public practically descended upon the stores to stock up on food and essentials after the authorities warned of an unexpected snowstorm on the US east coast.

Truth be told, none of us can completely feel protected because natural disasters like floods, hurricanes, and storms can happen suddenly and without much or any notice.

Purchasing emergency food supplies is similar to purchasing insurance in my opinion.

It's possible that we'll never see a war, a natural disaster, or a deadly new disease. We might, though. who is to say?

If that occurs, having access to food resources can be the difference between putting food on the table for your family and leaving them hungry.

You can feel secure in any circumstance if you have an emergency supply.

Water and food can help you stay calmer and avoid being overcome by panic, which will help you deal with the issue.

The ability to make yourself and your family independent for a few days until aid arrives and the ability to endure at least one short-term emergency situation unharmed are therefore vital.

Consequently, I want to assist you in becoming a prepper so that you can be prepared for the disaster that will occur at some point, whether it be a significant blackout, a new virus, wars similar to the ones we now have, or anything else that may occur soon. There is no avoiding it. Facts all around us support it.

People who are prepared for the end of life as we know it are called preppers. While the rest of the world is disintegrating, we preppers have access to emergency supplies, equipment, food, and locations where we can store all of these things.

It is a fairly common way of life for individuals to learn to withstand and overcome a variety of disasters of any kind. More and more of us are deciding to join the effort to safeguard ourselves and our families in the wake of the most recent economic crises, pandemics, and natural disasters.

The religious notion that the end of the world is approaching or the increased number of wars, upheavals, and riots that threaten to upend the status quo both inspire many people to engage in these behaviors.

The good news is that they can work in difficult circumstances if you have the required skills and tools. The need for this form of instruction has greatly increased. You've come to the proper place if you learned about this movement after going through a difficult moment and realizing you weren't prepared for it.

Truth be told, not all preparedness enthusiasts are prepared to share our identities or the safety precautions we have put in place. We take this precaution because we worry that in the event of a calamity, the unprepared will come after us and try to loot us.

This book is simply one introduction to all a prepper may do; you will discover the fundamentals of food preparation, preservation, and long-term conservation techniques here. The idea is that you will keep the essentials in large numbers in your safe place so your family will be well fed for a long period.

If you persevere and read all of my books, you will eventually be able to prepare food and shelter, defend yourself against harm and predators, make fire, identify the tools you'll need, maintain drinking water, and do everything else you'll need to take care of your loved ones, including your children and grandchildren.

In this book, I'll cover the essential things you should stockpile as well as stockpiling techniques, such as obtaining water, which is the first thing you think of when you want to be ready for the unavoidable.

To avoid illnesses and poisoning, I'll assist you locate sources of drinking water. To ensure that you don't run out of what is in storage when you are shut down, you will need to acquire drinking water, keep it in the bunker, and have filters.

The non-perishable goods, long-lasting foods that are good for storing, canned meats and fish, sugar, honey, pasta, rice, nuts, and dried fruits and vegetables will all be covered.

Simply put, this first volume in the collection will assist you in learning some of the fundamentals of prepping. When you have all of my books, you will be equipped to survive and won't need to worry about being caught off guard by any of the catastrophes that will undoubtedly occur, sooner or later.

Chapter 2

ESSENTIAL FOODS TO STOCK

To protect yourself and your family when it's time to lock yourself in, whether it's due to a nuclear attack, a war like the ones going on in the world right now, or a virus that isolates us, you must understand what foods you should have in your home or bunker. This knowledge is provided in the first chapter.

I'll go over what you must have and how to get it.

Emergency Provisions Kit

Having an emergency bag with food and other essentials is the first thing you should do in case something happens and you need to respond quickly.

What would you do if you were told to leave your home in the event of a disaster or "shelter-in-place" (remain at home until further notice)? Are you prepared to provide for your family's requirements till assistance arrives? The Federal Emergency Management Agency advises that you keep sufficient food, water, and other supplies on hand to survive on your own for at least three days because emergency services and local authorities cannot reach everyone promptly.

In spite of the fact that my goal is for you to survive far longer than simply three days, I'll discuss the current equipment in this section and then demonstrate how to sustain it in later sections. We are likely to lock ourselves inside for a very long period and struggle to survive if things continue the way they are. Preparation is necessary in this situation.

Disaster supplies include goods you could need before help arrives. If you want to be able to carry these goods with you if authorities order you to leave your home, pack them in portable containers (such wallets or tiny garbage cans). The location of the kit should be known to every member of your family.

Water should be your first purchase.

For drinking and cleaning purposes, each individual should keep 4 liters of water on hand each day. Although individual needs may differ, the typical daily requirement for drinking water is 2 liters. More water is required by young people, nursing moms, and the ill. Water demand may quadruple at very high temperatures.

The best way to store water is to keep it in its original, sealed packaging when you buy bottled water. A different option is to keep drinking water in sterile plastic beverage containers or sealed food storage containers (not in milk or juice bottles or cartons). With soap and water, properly wash these containers. To disinfect plastic drink bottles, mix one quart of water with one tablespoon of unscented home chlorine bleach. Shaking and then rinsing with fresh water are the proper ways to handle the solution's bottle. Add 2 drops of unscented liquid household chlorine bleach to non-chlorinated water (such as well water) before using it. Every six months, non-commercial bottled water needs to be changed.

Nonperishable foods that don't need refrigeration, cooking, water, or other specific preparation should be kept in 3-day supplies by each member of your home. Additionally, you could require specific foods for babies, persons with dietary restrictions, and animals.

Think about the subsequent storage configurations:

protein bars

tinned goods that are ready to eat, as well as fruits, meats, and vegetables.

Butter and jam with peanuts.

Dry cereals or granola.

Nuts.

a dried fruit.

Cookies that are salty and sweet.

Sweets.

Sugar, salt, and pepper.

tea and coffee instants.

Vitamins.

Baby food, elderly individuals also have needs in addition to their meals.

In case it's required, pet food.

Regularly replace any food that has expired in your first aid kit.

Include a can opener in your supply kit as well, don't forget.

air, the

You might need to filter your air when there is an emergency, such as when there are explosions or bioterrorist strikes. Wear a mask or a thick cotton garment (such as many cotton T-shirts) taped over your mouth or nose to do this. Drug stores sell snug-fitting face masks.

Sealing windows, doors, and vents can assist protect the space from contaminants from the outside if you are required to stay inside. As a result, your kit needs to have scissors, duct tape, and a heavy-duty plastic bag or sheet.

The last point is that while an air purifier with a high-efficiency particulate air filter can assist remove dust, mold, fumes, biological agents, and other impurities, it cannot completely stop chemical fumes.

Acute Care

You can aid in the recovery of various wounds with the materials found in the most basic first aid kit. Life-threatening situations, however, demand the attention of a medical specialist. If someone stops breathing or starts bleeding heavily, call for aid. Of course, this only applies in situations where the surroundings permit it. If not, I still urge you to enroll in some first aid classes and take whatever step you can to both assist others and assist yourself.

In your first aid pack, you should include the following supplies:

antiseptic 2-inch triangular rolled bandages in three rolls.

sterilized gauze pads in sizes 2 and 4.

Two pairs of latex gloves as well as additional pairs of sterile gloves, just in case.

different sized bandages.

Needles.

Tweezers.

Analgesics, antacids, laxatives, and other over-the-counter drugs for pain, diarrhea, and other conditions.

Antiseptic.

wet towels.

soap or cleaning supplies.

Scissors.

bobby pins.

Two tongue relaxers.

Thermometer.

Medications on prescription, though you should periodically check the expiration date.

gadget for measuring blood pressure or glucose.

Not to be forgotten if you require special items

In a crisis, some individuals could require specialized supplies. Infants may require formula, diapers, bottles, wipes, and other supplies. Elderly folks and those with impairments or medical illnesses may require extra eyeglasses, hearing aid batteries, wheelchair batteries, a list of prescription medications with dosages, and a list of medical devices (such pacemakers) with model and serial numbers. Consult a health care practitioner for assistance with emergency preparedness if you or a member of your family is using complex drugs (such as injectable medications, nebulizers, or dialysis).

Every member of your family should have a change of clothing and shoes, and your first aid kit should also contain a sleeping bag or blanket, a flashlight, a radio or television that runs on batteries, spare batteries that haven't expired, a whistle, cashier's or traveler's checks, hygiene supplies like toilet paper, bleach, and disinfectant, and copies of important papers like your driver's license, credit cards, and insurance. If you reside in a chilly climate, pack additional blankets, warm clothing, caps, gloves, scarves, and coats. Find out what else your family members could require in an emergency by talking to them all.

It's a good idea to keep some supplies in your office and car because you never know when a tragedy will hit. Bring food and drink with you to work, along with a pair of comfy shoes in case you need to be evacuated. If you're unable to go home, the provisions in your car—including food, water, first-aid kits, flares, jumper cables, and station supplies—can help you fulfill your demands.

Finally, a quick list of the components of a basic disaster supply kit follows:

Whistle.

a sealed canister of matches.

supplies for hygiene.

a wrench or pliers

handbook and first aid kit.

radio with a TV battery.

Scissors.

tape for insulation.

or plastic sheets or sacks.

a dust mask or cotton that absorbs.

foods that won't spoil quickly.

animal supplies

itemized special needs.

copies of crucial paperwork

opening a can

tools for the kitchen.

additional footwear and clothing

This would be the kit to take care of urgent demands, but I want to show you how to have one for longer durations, where you might have to shut yourself up for a while. The things you need to have are listed below.

Stockpiling 20 Survival Items

All of them are simple and will frequently be of assistance. Perhaps you take them for granted now, but in the event of a disaster, they will be invaluable if there is an emergency.

Batteries are essential; rechargeable batteries can be very helpful, but alkaline batteries provide a backup option in the event of a power outage. In the long term, though, you might decide to get those more expensive than alkaline batteries because they will perform well in the device you use them in.

The suggestion I give you is to test every battery your equipment requires before making a purchase, unlike the alkaline batteries ruined by rust.

Flasks and lighters

In an emergency, you can use a flashlight to illuminate and dissuade assailants. Because they are not required to carry bulky, heavy flashlights for their illumination needs, preppers find it easier. Most tactical flashlights are lightweight and robust. It can be quite helpful to wear a flashlight.

Along with the traditional lighter, the lighter has advantages when used with matches. When you need to light up and there is no electricity, this will be crucial.

You may also get lighters that look like a stick and contain a specific chemical that won't burn out when exposed to water or sand.

sanitary napkins, wipes

You might put seeds in the cardboard tubes if you had supplies of wipes, paper towels, and toilet paper, which are necessities for survival even after they run out.

Energy, solar power, and generators

The problem of electricity is a fundamental one. Many preparedness enthusiasts use gas-powered generators as a backup source of electricity, but it's possible that these essential fuels won't be available.

In the event of a calamity, switch to solar generators and store energy in rechargeable batteries.

Consider which electrical options would be most advantageous over the long run.

Adhesive and insulating tapes All Types of Tapes

You have a very practical and adaptable tool in insulating tape. With it, you can mend a lot of problems. The first recommendation is to keep it away from heat, as it will cause it to become sticky and worthless.

Have tape on hand for repairing, tying off, and wrapping cables. There are many different types of tapes, so my recommendation is that you carry a little quantity of each so you can address any problem.

Lighters

They are built of various materials and are used to start a fire quickly. Some ignite when you scrape them on charcoal or sticks, while others light even while wet, allowing you to have them and start a fire in even the trickiest situations.

Ropes If you need to lay something or tie something down so it won't fall, climb a steep canyon wall, or any other difficult terrain, you'll need a rope. Furthermore, different varieties of rope are required for different tasks when performing heavy duty operations.

It is vital to use candles. If a nuclear disaster occurs, you won't be able to predict when you'll have power or light once more, and you have no assurance that the batteries would last forever. The candles are there to provide light. You can purchase some that are designed for survival and last a lot of hours, giving you a period of light that is guaranteed.

Seeds After a disaster, it's possible that people won't be able to raise crops or engage in trade. The supermarket does not carry grains. To be able to cultivate your own food and not be only dependent on what you have saved in the bunker, you must have seeds.

Insect Repellents

You don't know exactly what is happening to you or for how long you will be locked down now that you are cooped up; you don't want to get bitten by a swarm of mosquitoes right now and end up with an illness. You and the people you care about will be in better health if you take precautions against these insects.

Propane Gas, Kerosene, Butane Gas

In order for you to cook, you are going to need access to a variety of fuels, such as propane gas and butane, among others.

Canvas and Blankets

All of the valuables in your shelter will be protected by the tarp. You won't have to worry about your tent ripping or falling apart even if you're camped out on rough terrain. In addition to that, you can use it to catch rainwater and throw things that are heavier.

Various Types of Bags

Plastic bags are not only effective at keeping water out in the event that you forget your sleeping bag, but you can also stuff them with dry leaves to make them more comfortable for your back. It is a good idea to store certain foods and items in airtight bags. It is beneficial to have them available in a variety of sizes.

Chlorine and other Decontaminants

Bleach is going to be useful for a wide variety of different options. In addition to making the water suitable for drinking, this will also help disinfect the surfaces on which food is prepared.

Assorted Nails and Screws

The screws and nails will be of assistance to you in maintaining the security of the areas; perhaps you need to mend some wood, or there was an earthquake that knocked things down, and you need to tie various elements that you need to protect. You simply cannot fathom how important screws and nails are in this predicament, and on top of that, they occupy very little room.

Raw honey that has not been filtered.

Raw honey is superior to pasteurized honey in terms of health benefits, flavor, and impact on the environment. By purchasing organic honey, you can ensure that you will not be exposed to any pesticides that may have been sprayed on or near plants that were visited by bees.

Consume raw honey because it will provide you with nourishment for a very long time.

Fishing Rope or Line

When you are stranded and in need of protein to eat, all you need is some patience, a fishing line, and some bait that you can get out of a can. You will be successful in catching fish. There are a variety of fishing lines that I strongly suggest you have in your arsenal. Do not be content with just one; rather, select several so that they can be used for a longer period of time and the whole family can fish.

Chapter 3

Several Instruments for Making and Fixing Things

These items are essential to have in your bunker:

Hammer: The use of a carpenter's hammer is absolutely necessary. Try to find models that are ergonomic, preferably with wooden handles. There is a wide range of prices; if you are unsure which model to buy, find out what the average price is, and check to see if you are able to manage its weight.

Sandpaper: Sandpaper can be purchased in a variety of forms. You will need the most coarse and the most fine (the latter is usually used for finishing). One of the most common applications for sandpaper is to rough up walls in preparation for painting. For the sanding process to go more smoothly, you might also require holders for the sandpaper in a variety of sizes.

Look for screwdriver sets if you need additional screwdrivers. It is essential to have both a flat head and a Phillips' head at your disposal. Check that the handles are comfortable to use by ensuring that they are ergonomic. Even screwdrivers with magnets built in are available.

Make sure that the handle of the cutter can be retracted. It will be of the utmost benefit for cutting cardboard, among other materials, as well as for opening cardboard.

A collection of wrenches: It can be put to a wide variety of uses. Wrenches can come in a variety of sizes, so it's best to look for a set of wrenches rather than just one.

A box of tools: Maintaining order across the board should be a priority. Toolboxes are available in numerous sizes and designs. There are even toolboxes that have multiple functions already built into them. Other tools and supplies that might come in handy around the house include surface protectors in case you need to paint or sand, a saw or handsaw, brushes, rollers, and so on.

Armement, including Knives and Arrows

Everyone's top priority when the world is turned upside down is to stay alive. There are some people who, like you, want to provide their loved ones with the best possible protection, food, and safety at home. Others, those who give in to chaos; you have to take precautions to protect yourself in case any threats materialize. Not only people but also animals could show up, particularly if you have no choice but to leave your house.

Attacking a bobcat does not necessarily require you to have an AK-47 in your possession. For instance, you can equip yourself with a bow and arrow, knives of varying sizes and quality that are sharpened to a fine edge, knife sharpeners, and anything else that you deem necessary for your protection while hunting.

Now that you are aware of the things that you should have, let's talk about the food that you should put in the bunker, specifically those foods that have a long shelf life.

You Should Begin Storing These Ten Foods for Survival Before It Is Too Late

You need to immediately go out and purchase these foods, then immediately put them away in the bunker. My recommendation is that you get ones with a date of expiration that is far in the future, and make sure you keep track of when those dates are so that you can rotate them. I will get back to you on that later. The following is some information on the foods you ought to consume and the reasons why.

Activated Oat Groats

Oat sprouts can be added to breakfast cereal, salads, or used to make plant-based milk, which is both more nutritious and more easily digestible. Oat sprouts can also be used to make any other food. You can obtain this superfood by allowing it to grow into oat grass and then juicing it, dehydrating it, and then grinding it into a powder. It has a high concentration of chlorophyll in addition to amino acids, enzymes, and vitamins. In addition to being high in antioxidants, it is also used as a treatment for hormonal imbalances and menopausal symptoms because of the phytochemicals it contains.

Oat sprouts are packed with protein and beta-glucan, both of which have been shown to reduce levels of cholesterol in the blood.

Because they contain both soluble and insoluble fiber, they are also prebiotic, meaning that they encourage the growth of beneficial bacteria in the digestive tract.

Oats, in general, are beneficial for the digestive system as a whole. Acquaint yourself with the qualities of oats as well as the effects they have on one's health.

Liquor

You won't be storing the liquor so that you can drink it during the celebration, which is something that might strike you as odd. It can be used to sterilize surfaces, keep food fresh, and even clean wounds,... and why not, every once in a while, have a little taste... However, the fact of the matter is that alcoholic beverages have many applications when you are in survival mode.

Apple Cider Vinegar as the Subject

Although apple cider vinegar is most well-known for its use as a salad dressing, it also has a wide variety of applications in the fields of home care, beauty, and wellness. According to conventional wisdom, it is an essential component of all different kinds of home remedies, ranging from the treatment of acne and acne scarring to the treatment of weight loss and sore throats. I will demonstrate to you how to make use of it.

Vinegar made from apple cider has been used medicinally since 3300 B.C., when its benefits were first discovered. Since Hippocrates, who is widely regarded as the "father of medicine," used apple cider vinegar as a healing elixir, antibiotic, and general health tonic, the practice has been around for four hundred years.

Apple cider vinegar is distinguished by the presence of a high concentration of a variety of nutrients, including vitamins A, C, E, and B complex, bioflavonoids, acetic acid, propionic acid, lactic acid, enzymes, amino acids, potassium, calcium, magnesium, phosphorus, sodium, iron, and copper.

Powdered Milk

When milk is dehydrated, it loses about 80 percent of its weight, making it easier to store for a longer period of time. Because of this, its storage and transportation costs are reduced as a result of its reduced size.

Because of this, you can think of it as a necessary food item in situations where there is no electricity and insufficient recooling, such as in a bunker. In 1980, imported milk powder was a significant contender in developing countries' markets.

Not only can it be stored for extended periods of time, but we can do so in a variety of different settings, not just factories or warehouses. In addition to that, mountaineers, hikers, nomads, mountain farmers, mountaineers, and even the military all make extensive use of it. This is due to the fact that it does not need to be refrigerated and that it can be transported easily in large quantities. You should not deny yourself having it, and if you combine it with cereal, you will have a breakfast that is both filling and nourishing.

Products Stored in Cans and Crackers

When foods are stored or cooked, they undergo change; however, the variables that affect nutrient loss in industrial processes are highly controlled, and as a result, there is typically less loss of nutrients in industrially processed foods than there is in freshly prepared or processed foods that are prepared at home.

The temperatures that are used in canning food may cause the food to lose some of its nutritional value.

Because the temperature in industrial processes is carefully selected to preserve the flavor, color, and odor characteristics of the food, the answer is no. Following the canning process, the product goes through a heat sterilization procedure, in which it is heated to between 120 and 130 degrees Celsius for a brief period of time (less than 30 minutes). This process deactivates the enzymes in the food, which stops its maturation. As a result, the loss of nutrients that would have occurred due to the lack of oxygen and the lack of contact between the product and the outside environment is slowed down (solid, liquid, gaseous substances and even light). The majority of the food in your kit will be in canned form; however, this will not be the only type of food included, so you will be aware of all the alternatives.

Protein Powder

In recent years, protein powder has emerged as one of the most popular dietary supplements, and research has shown that taking it regularly, in addition to maintaining a healthy diet and getting plenty of exercise, can help you see noticeable changes in your body in a short amount of time. However, it is essential to have a thorough understanding of how to consume protein powder and what foods should be consumed alongside it. Before beginning to consume it, you should always think about both the positive and negative effects it may have on your body.

You will be able to maintain your health, maintain your nutrition, and make the most of every resource that the bunker has to offer if you consume this protein. You can never be sure how long it will keep working for you.

You will find that one of the benefits is that it will speed up your metabolism.

Helps you lose weight and keeps it off.

It is helpful for the development of muscles.

It controls your appetite. You could eat it as a snack in between the main courses of your meals.

Boosts levels of the happy hormone serotonin.

Helps to calm the nerves.

Water and Water Filters

The water that is delivered to our house is of a quality that is suitable for consumption. But in the event that something catastrophic takes place, we will have to use the water that we have stored. Even though water can be stored in containers, its freshness will not be preserved indefinitely. You are required to make use of rainwater and filter the water you obtain, as it may contain bacteria, viruses, and toxic substances such as lead, fluoride, lime, and chlorine. There is a diverse selection of water filters available, some of which are tailored to remove particular types of contaminants.

Salts, minerals, and organic matter are all components of water; purification systems remove any unwanted or potentially harmful components. Activated carbon, ultraviolet (UV) lamps, and ion exchange resins are the three primary components that are typically used in purification systems. Activated carbon is used to remove contaminants, UV lamps remove microorganisms, and ion exchange resins remove minerals and metals.

Grains

Cereal grains include wheat, oats, rye, and rice, as well as chickpeas and beans, amongst other foods. Grains are the seeds of cereals. Consuming them provides the body with fiber, minerals, and vitamins. These will provide you with the nutrients and fill you up that you need. Consuming a plate of lentils, rather than a good steak, will provide you with a greater amount of protein.

Rice

Rice is essential for the preparation of food reserves in the event that a catastrophe or unforeseen circumstances occur. White rice is one of the foods that is (almost always) available here. Raw rice, similar to honey, has an exceptionally low moisture content; consequently, rice that has been vacuum-sealed can remain edible for a significant amount of time. This works for white, wild, jasmine, or basmati rice, but not for brown rice, which has a shelf life of no more than one year due to the high oil content of brown rice. In addition, if stored properly, pasta can maintain its freshness for decades. It is possible to store it in its dry state for up to ten years at a stable ambient temperature of approximately 21 degrees. The shelf life is proportionally increased when temperatures are lowered.

Multivitamins

Last but not least, I suggest taking a multivitamin, which is a supplement that consists of various vitamins, minerals, and other nutritional components.

They can typically be obtained in the form of capsules, tablets, powders, or liquids. In general, the purpose of these supplements is to treat vitamin deficiencies brought on by conditions such as digestive disorders, in specific circumstances such as pregnancy, and even in some cases by a diet that is deficient in nutrients.

These vitamins and minerals are found naturally in foods and should be part of a balanced diet; however, when circumstances do not allow it, it is then appropriate to get them through other means; supplements can help you.

There are twelve types of food that can be stored for a long time.

Take into consideration these foods that can be stored for a lifetime or a significant number of years.

Sachet Drinks

When combined with water, fruit juice powder becomes a drinkable powdered concentrate that has the flavor of fruit. It is available in a wide range of flavors, including both single-fruit and mixed flavors, and is packaged in plastic bags of a single serving size. They are frequently referred to as single juices in common parlance. [Citation needed]

Ingredients include fruit juice that has been dehydrated, acidulants such as citric acid, flavorings, anti-caking agents such as tricalcium phosphate, and colorants such as tartrazine or titanium dioxide.

Sweeteners are used in so-called powdered juices, which come in both regular and low-calorie varieties. Although the laws that permit their use differ from country to country, aspartame, acesulfame potassium, cyclamate, and saccharin are all acceptable alternatives to sugar.

Because they are subjected to a great deal of processing, they have a lengthy shelf life. Even though they are not exactly the poster child for good health, it is never a bad idea to have some in your bunker because you can get a wide variety of fruits and flavors in them.

White Vinegar

Is the white vinegar the same as the cleaning vinegar even though they look very similar and have very similar names? It is in its beginnings, but not in its present-day applications and functions. Glucose derived from sugar cane, corn, or malt undergoes a two-step fermentation process to produce white vinegar. This process produces alcohol and acetic acid.

At first, white vinegar was utilized in the kitchen as a sour sauce that could be used on a variety of dishes, including salads. In later years, white cleaning vinegar was developed as a result of the numerous cleaning applications of white vinegar. As a result, cleaning vinegar is a subcategory of white vinegar that is formulated to both disinfect and clean.

One of these vinegars, white vinegar, can be consumed while the other, cleaning vinegar, cannot; this is the primary distinction between the two. This is primarily as a result of the acidity of it. White vinegar has an acidity level that ranges between 3% and 5%, whereas cleaning vinegar has an acidity level of 8%, making the latter more appropriate for use in cleaning applications but rendering it inedible.

If stored in an area that is moderately cool, white vinegar has a shelf life that extends into the decades.

Canning

There is a "best before" date printed on the label of every can of food. However, this date can be used as a safety measure to prevent food poisoning because the food is likely to remain in good condition after this point in time.

Canned foods have a shelf life that ranges from one to six years, as stated by the Food and Drug Administration of the United States;

however, it is believed that they can stay in good condition for up to one hundred years.

How to Determine If Canned Food Is Still Good to Eat

The botulinum toxin is the most common type of food poisoning that people get from eating spoiled food that has been canned. This toxin can live without oxygen. Even though it is extremely uncommon, this disease is fatal.

Even so, it is best to err on the side of caution and make sure everything is in order before consuming the food, particularly if the can is very old or has been exposed to high temperatures. Botox, fortunately, generates a gas that expands the cans and makes it simpler to recognize the contents within each one. Do not try any of the contents of the can if you find that it has expanded, or if it appears or smells spoiled. Instead, just throw it away.

Tomato Powder

Tomato powder is an excellent, flavorful, and extremely versatile ingredient that can be used in a wide variety of cooking applications. It is simple to prepare, and it is very effective for preserving tomatoes and saving space. If you grow tomatoes during the summer, you may find that you suddenly have an abundance of tomatoes, to the point where you are at a loss for how to use them all. Wouldn't it be wonderful if you could store those delicious tomatoes for the rest of the year and for a much longer period of time? It would be wonderful if you could learn how to dry tomatoes for the purpose of preserving them as well as how to make tomato powder to use in the dishes that you enjoy cooking the most.

Salt

The question "Does salt heal?" might be more appropriate. The mineral sodium chloride, more commonly known as salt, is essential to the health and function of the human body as well as the bodies of all other animals. However, an excess of it can be harmful to the body even though it assists in maintaining the body's fluid levels. Salt is a natural ingredient that can be found both on land and in the sea. It has been utilized for a variety of purposes ever since ancient times. It has been used for a very long time to impart flavor to food and to preserve it.

In contrast to many other seasonings, salt does not have a predetermined expiration date but rather a date by which it should be used. After the expiration date, you can safely use regular table salt or sea salt to add flavor and satisfy your requirements. Other types of salts, such as rock salt, curing salts, and bath salts, are also suitable for use over extended periods of time.

When exposed to moisture or steam, old salt can form a crust or become more rigid.

A pantry is an ideal location for storing salt because of its cool, dark environment and airtight container that it came in. It is imperative that this be kept dry at all times. It is also preferable to maintain a constant temperature, and to do so in a location that is not near the oven or the dishwasher.

Spices

Spices and dried herbs do not have an indefinite shelf life; however, they do not need to be replaced on a monthly basis, and in most cases, they will even remain usable for several years. They do not go bad to an unhealthy degree or reach their expiration date. However, over time, a significant period of time, they lose some of their properties. As a result, it is necessary to renew them in order for them to continue to provide the organism with aroma, flavor, and benefits.

Spices are plants that have been dried out. To assist in the process of food preservation and to inhibit the growth of bacteria, an extraction process using water is utilized. The shelf life of these food additives is extremely long; however, this does vary depending on the type of food additive and the manner in which it is stored.

Pet Food

It is possible for pet food to remain good for a very long time; for instance, when it is sold in a bag, it can remain good for up to two years; at least, that is what is typically stated on the bag, but it can remain good for even longer. When it is canned, the date of expiration that is typically marked on the jar is two years in the future.

Dry feed is not immune to the spoiling effects of food over time. It goes without saying that you can't evaluate the quality of food based on its aroma. The smell of many pet foods, especially wet cat food, is off-putting to human noses.

On the other hand, if you are accustomed to a specific brand or kind of food, you will notice that the product has a different aroma after it has passed its expiration date.

Beans They are also known as chickpeas, fava beans, and other similar names. If the drying process is carried out properly, they have the potential to last for up to thirty years. It is important to remember that in order to store them for an extended period of time, they need to be vacuum packed and shielded from light.

Rice that's White

At least five years of storage time is available for white rice, and even more time is available if it is vacuum packed. The storage conditions, along with a list of other types of rice, are provided in the following paragraph. Rice's shelf life is determined by a variety of factors, including the type of rice, whether or not it has been cooked, how it has been packaged, and how it has been stored.

Rice is the most important staple food for the majority of the world's population, and it provides more than one-fifth of the calories that are consumed by humans all over the world.

Rice, much like pasta, can be found in a wide variety of forms (white, brown, wild, short-grain, long-grain, etc.) and is frequently flavored with a variety of herbs and seasonings. It should come as no surprise that billions of people around the world consume it on a daily basis given that it has a low overall cost, a high caloric density, a long shelf life, and a high nutritional value. On the other hand, not all types of rice are the same. How long can white rice, brown rice, or wild rice be stored once it has been opened?

When stored in oxygen-free containers at a temperature of 4 degrees Celsius or lower, refined white rice has a shelf life of up to 30 years. If they are not stored appropriately, all foods will, of course, have a shorter shelf life. It is important to keep in mind, however, that both white and brown rice, in addition to a large number of other types of grains, typically have a lengthy shelf life. Therefore, you are able to continue using it without risk after the date of expiration.

Oats

This grain contains a significant amount of fiber. Because it helps to keep cholesterol in check, it can be incorporated into one's regular diet and even used as a stand-in for flour in some recipes. It can be kept for up to four months in a cool, dry place if it is sealed tightly in an airtight container and kept there. Since it does not expire, there is no reason for you to be without it in your bunker.

Pickles Pickles are yet another tasty and intriguing food choice. Vinegar-marinated vegetables are a handy food that can be consumed at any time and stored for a considerable amount of time. It is recommended that pickles be stored in sealed glass jars, in regions with low humidity, and away from refrigerators. This is standard practice in the field of canning.

Nuts in their natural state, without any additions such as honey or oil, are another type of food that may be stored for a long time and still be consumed without any problems, provided that the nuts do not show any indications that they are in poor condition.

If you want to be able to keep them for a long time, the best way to do so is to put them in a dark, dry place inside of a glass container that is airtight and then place that container inside of the case.

If you want to restore the full potential of the fruit after it has lost some of its texture, flavor, and scent, here are some tips:

Utilize natural antioxidants, such as lemon, which, in addition to containing citric acid, is also a good source of vitamin C. Other natural sources of antioxidants include green tea, cacao, and berries.

You should dicing it up and store it in a Tupperware container, ensuring that the container is airtight by making sure it is hermetically sealed.

You could also put it in a vacuum bag that can be sealed back up again.

Keep the fruit cut up and stored in a container with some cold water. You may also add some white vinegar or lemon juice to the mixture.

Wrap the fruit in a damp napkin, and then place it in a Tupperware container that has a lid that can be hermetically sealed.

The olive oil

Olive oil has a shelf life of anywhere from 18 to 36 months, depending on the type of olive oil and whether or not it has been filtered. Olive oil can stay fresh and in good condition for this long. From the moment the wine is bottled until it is consumed, the ideal window is no longer than nine months, as recommended by industry professionals. It is still possible for it to last for many years. The use-by dates are merely a guide, as I explained to you previously.

If the olive oil is filtered, it has a shelf life of up to two years; however, its lifespan is cut in half if it is exposed to high temperatures, air, or light, or if it is contaminated with bacteria during the filtering process. Because it has a higher concentration of pollutants, it will only be good for a few months if it is not filtered.

As long as the environmental conditions discussed earlier are maintained, extra virgin olive oil has a shelf life of anywhere from 18 months to three years. This is because it includes a higher concentration of antioxidants, which helps it maintain olive juice for a longer period of time. In any other case, it may endure for six months.

This Is Something That Will Last Forever: Food in Powder Form

I'm going to show you below how to make many of your favorite foods using a freeze-drying equipment. Each of the powdered foods has an indefinite shelf life and can be included into a variety of different dishes.

Egg Powder

Egg powder is a product that is utilized in the culinary sector that is derived from eggs. It consists of freshly laid eggs that have been shattered in a sanitary and mechanical manner. The resulting powder is then subjected to high-tech dehydration with stabilizers and then the pasteurization process.

Egg white powder, egg yolk powder, whole egg powder, and even mayonnaise powder are some examples of egg products that have been "powdered." These egg products are dehydrated in order to maintain their qualities for a longer period of time.

Egg powder is a more long-lasting product than fresh eggs, which means that you will have access to eggs for an extended period of time if you use it. Additionally, the price is lower than that of fresh eggs. It is more hygienic since it eliminates the drawbacks connected with it, such as the accumulation of dirt on the shells, the risk of contamination, and the attraction of insects.

When added to things like pasta or smoothies, it makes certain dishes far more convenient than using raw eggs would. It is widely used in commercial and industrial settings, but it is also gaining popularity in residential settings.

It is utilized in the baking of pastries, breads, and candies, in addition to other areas of the food business. You may make cupcakes, pastries, vanilla extract, spaghetti, bread, and a variety of other baked goods and foods using powdered eggs.

To utilize it effectively, the ratio of egg powder to water that you should follow is one part egg powder to three parts water.

Peanut Butter Powder

Pressing peanuts into a powder results in the production of peanut butter powder. Due to the fact that this method expels a considerable amount of oil, it might be utilized as a more nutritious substitute for conventional peanut butter. The consistency of powdered peanut butter, once reconstituted, is quite similar to that of traditional peanut butter, and the powder itself can be used in a wide variety of recipes. You may improve the flavor of dishes like granola and yogurt by adding the powder to them, or you can use it to replace some of the flour in baked goods. Both of these options are available. Peanut butter powder has the potential to be a valuable item both in the kitchen and in your bunker if the proper preparation method is used.

The best thing is that you can use it to enjoy this butter in recipes like granola with nuts and to add sweetness to food. You can also use it to enjoy it on its own.

Powdered Milk

I have already informed you about powdered milk, and now I would like to advise you to stock up on it while keeping a close eye on when it will go bad. You will have access to the calcium supplement in addition to everything else that milk offers, and it will also last you a very long time, significantly longer than if you consumed it in liquid form.

Hemp Powder

The seeds of the hemp plant are used to make the protein powder known as hemp protein. Because it tastes something like nuts, quite a few individuals enjoy the flavor of it.

In general, these plant proteins are simple for the body to break down. It should not come as a surprise that 91 to 98 percent of the constituents in hemp protein powders are digestible. This indicates that the body is able to utilize these components for essential processes.

A study that was conducted and published in the Journal of Agricultural and Food Chemistry found that hemp is simple to digest due to the presence of edestin and albumin in the plant. The body swiftly breaks down these proteins into their constituent amino acids.

Hemp seeds are a source of phosphorus, magnesium, calcium, iron, manganese, zinc, and copper, according to a study that was published in the journal Food and Function. The study was conducted on hemp seeds. In a similar vein, one serving of certain protein powders is guaranteed to include 80 percent of the recommended daily intake (RDI) of magnesium and 52 percent of the RDI of iron.

Baking Powder

The most beneficial aspect of baking powder is that, despite the fact that, in the event of a catastrophe, you won't be using the bunker oven to bake a cake, you may use it in its place to get the same results as baking soda.

Cocoa Powder

Cocoa powder is one of the most popular items that may be made from cocoa.

Cocoa powder is a food that is high in calories, is abundant in protein, is low in carbohydrates and fats (depending on how it is prepared), and is only partially saturated.

It is a good source of vitamins of the B group, as well as vitamins A and E. The contributions of minerals are diverse and include sources of potassium, phosphorus, iron, salt, magnesium, calcium, copper, manganese, zinc, and selenium, among other minerals.

Because of the high antioxidant content of cocoa, the contribution of stimulating alkaloids, and the contribution of euphoric phenethylamines, eating chocolate can make us feel happier. Cocoa has a high level of all three of these beneficial compounds. Having some will go a long way toward helping to ease the difficult times, particularly for youngsters.

The Ground Cinnamon

A variety of foods, including sweets, beverages, and infusions, can benefit from the use of cinnamon as a spice. This substance, which is used in cooking, contains features that help keep our bodies in good shape, and those properties help keep our bodies in good shape.

Cinnamon has even been used as a home medicine for thousands of years, and this is another food that lasts a long time in powdered form and is one that you absolutely must have with you. Cinnamon can be found in most grocery stores and health food stores.

Parmesan Powder

The same way that you already add taste to your meals with the Parmesan that you acquire from the grocery store, you can also add flavor to your meals with Parmesan powder, which is beneficial for preserving in powdered form as well.

Potato Flakes

Potato flakes, often known as quick mashed potatoes, are widely regarded as one of the most useful innovations in the annals of the food industry. This method supplants the conventional approach to consuming mashed potatoes. Edward Asselbergs, a Dutch-Canadian scientist, invented it in 1962 as a result of the findings of extensive study that involved the creation of a method that may extend the shelf life of some foods by dehydrating them.

In addition to being an excellent side dish for any dinner, mashed potatoes are an important component of a healthy diet since they contribute to the maintenance of a healthy weight when consumed in moderation.

Powder made from Chickpeas

The use of chickpea flour in place of standard wheat flour is both beneficial to one's health and delicious.

The high levels of fiber and vegetable protein that are found in chickpea flour are just two of the many advantages of using this type of flour. Intestinal transit is improved, and our bodies are better regulated as a result.

Gelatin

Gelatin is a tasteless and odorless material that is produced by extracting collagen from the bones and cartilage of animals. In the making of sweets, it is frequently utilized in the role of a gelling agent. In addition, it can be found in various foods acting in the capacity of a stabilizer or thickener.

Powder Made From Turmeric

The root of the plant is ground up and used to make the turmeric that we find on store shelves and in the spice section. Turmeric, once it has been processed, takes on a vivid yellow color, which has led many cultures to employ it as a dye. Curry powder also typically contains a good amount of turmeric powder as one of its components. Products like as capsules, teas, powders, and extracts containing turmeric are all available for purchase on the market today.

The key component in turmeric is called curcumin, and it possesses tremendous biological characteristics. Ayurvedic medicine is a traditional kind of Indian medicine that promotes the consumption of turmeric as a treatment for a wide range of illnesses.

Chronic pain and inflammation are two of these symptoms. It is beneficial to have turmeric's qualities on hand in the bunker because Western medicine has recently began researching turmeric as a potential therapy and pain reliever.

Garlic Powder

Garlic is hand-selected, peeled, sliced, and then dehydrated to make this product. Because it is such an effective preservative, in addition to being used for flavoring preparations, it is also commonly employed in the making of sausages.

Garlic powder has a more nuanced and powerful flavor than raw garlic, but it does not have the tingling feeling that raw garlic does. It is recommended that this product be kept in a dry and cold location.

Wheat Flour

In batters, cookies, and cakes, corn flour is often used as an auxiliary flour because it lends a touch of sweetness to the finished product. Baking is a good use for it; for instance, you might incorporate it into the dough for biscuits.

Golden Glucose

Baking, seasoning, and glazing are among possible use for light brown sugar. For instance, gingerbread, which is known for its robust molasses flavor, calls for the use of dark brown sugar. Your bunker should be able to preserve it for a significant amount of time.

Corn Starch Corn starch is used in a variety of culinary applications, including cooking, food preparation, baking, and confectionery. One of the characteristics of corn starch is that it acts as a thickening agent. Individuals diagnosed with celiac disease are able to consume meals containing cornstarch.

You should now know how to start building up your food reserves, the first steps to getting food from scratch, and how to learn how to organize them in your space. Now that you know what foods you could have and which ones last longer, you should know how you can begin to build up your food reserves.

Chapter 4

BEGIN RIGHT NOW TO COMPILE YOUR FOOD STASH FROM SCRATCH

The stockpiling of food must be done in an organized manner. It may be simple, but ensuring that it is carried out correctly is essential. I'm going to walk you through the process of getting started with hoarding and give you some important pointers.

Several Varieties of Available Stockpiles

You must have these stocks in your portfolio:

Both Food and Water

Preppers have known for a long time that one of the ways to get ready for the end of the world is to store away supplies of food and services that can endure for many years.

If the packaging is done correctly, some items can be preserved for years or even decades.

Remember the list of meals that I provided for you as an illustration before; keep it in mind as you are preparing your survival space.

Tools are another category of essential items. I'm going to run down a few of them for you:

Instruments that aid with labor.

Cutlery and other weapons.

Ropes in their various forms.

Fire starters.

All different kinds of pliers.

Power supply options.

Lamps.

Toolbox organizers and dividers

Silicone gun.

Medications and basic first aid supplies.

How to Get Started with Your Food and Water Stockpile

If we are given the task of preserving food for the longest amount of time possible, the first thing that comes to everyone's mind is to stock up on cans of every imaginable variety.

This method of food preservation was developed at the direct request of the French government during the Napoleonic wars. At that time, the French government offered a reward of 12,000 francs to any inventor who could devise a method that was both cost-effective and effective in preserving large quantities of food. Nicolas Appert, an oenologist, was declared the winner of the competition because he discovered a way to prevent the effects of microbes in food fifty years prior to the time when Louis Pasteur, another Frenchman, identified his part in all of this.

Even while they perform roughly the same function as Appert's original cans and are excellent solutions for the long-term preservation of food, the modern versions of these cans are a great deal more complex than the originals. Remember that we are hoarding supplies in preparation for a post-apocalyptic scenario, therefore it is in our best interest to choose highly processed foods that have the highest concentration of nutrients and calories if we are going to rely on canned goods.

Another fantastic resource are meals that have been freeze-dried.

It may appear as though a massive bunker stocked with cans would be an excellent tool for surviving the apocalypse, but we will need significantly more space to store freeze-dried foods and other varieties of tinned items.

This method of preservation is a process called dehydration, which does not require heat, hence avoiding nutritional and sensory losses to a considerable extent. You can freeze-dry nearly anything you want, and you can prepare individual packs of freeze-dried food so that you can keep track of everyone's nutrition and make sure that everyone gets the same amount. There are ways to heat the meal without the need for an external power source; in fact, the military of many different countries already have it, so there is no problem even if you do not have electricity.

The availability of water poses a challenge for these foods, which makes our survival in this post-apocalyptic world that much more difficult.

We Cannot Ignore the Importance of Water
Even though vast quantities of food can be preserved in cans, if a food is very energizing, it indicates that it is very concentrated in nutrients, and this means that it has very little moisture.

In these post-apocalyptic days, water will be the limiting factor. We are always thinking about conserving food, but someone needs to remember to carry purification tablets, and we also need to figure out a means to make drinking water out of salt water. In addition to this, the ocean provides a rich source of nutrients, as well as a substantial amount of edible seaweed.

Putting milk in the fridge is another wonderful choice. In addition to providing you with essential nutrients, it is packed with a lot of water. In this situation, my recommendation is to have a sufficient amount of drinking water stored in containers. In addition, please remember to bring water purifiers with you, as I mentioned earlier.

Establish Both a Short-Term and Long-Term Food Supply

To ensure both a short-term and a long-term supply of food, you will need to follow these measures. The length of time that the meal can be stored makes a difference. The following are some suggestions:

You should plan your purchases as much as possible.

You need to prepare a short-term menu (for example, for the next 15 days) that includes breakfast, lunch, snacks, and dinner, taking into consideration the number of people, in order to determine how much food each of them will require (which includes minor ingredients). such as garlic, onion, oil, etc.) and the appropriate dosage for us to follow. For example, if the 15-day menu calls for chickpea stew for four people, you should put additional ingredients like a bag of frozen spinach and a piece of salted cod in your dish.

Purchase Foods That Have a Long Shelf Life

Bring along some food that can be stored for an extended period of time, such as foods in cans or powdered form, as well as anything else that can be stored in your pantry for a number of months or even years.

How to Get Your Pantry in Order While Staying Within Your Financial Means

There are a lot of web pages that break down all of the many keys to avoiding famine during a disaster. The Federal Emergency Management Agency, which is assigned with the responsibility of reacting to these extreme crises that are hitting the United States, advises the following shopping list.

Find your space, to begin with.

Find a space in your house that is cold, dry, and dark; a storage room, basement, or garage area are typically the best options. If you do not have access to that option, you can begin removing items from the larger closet that you have. The selection of space is quite important because purchases will be made according to the capacity of the area. As soon as you have everything figured out, it is time to go shopping.

Water

Keep in mind that there is no such thing as having too much. The Federal Emergency Management Agency (FEMA) suggests stockpiling at least three liters of water per person, per day, for each individual's supply. However, keep in mind that needs vary according to age, physical condition, exercise level, food, and climate. These factors all play a role. Children, nursing mothers, and those who are sick require a greater amount. Extremely high temperatures will cause the amount necessary to double. In the event of a medical emergency, additional water might be necessary.

How should one store? It is strongly suggested that you purchase bottled water, which should then be kept sealed in its original packaging until it is time to be consumed. Consider the length of the product's shelf life.

Food Stay away from foods that stimulate your appetite for liquids. Pick cereals made with full grains, unsalted crackers, and canned items with plenty of fluids. Be sure to stock up on dry mixes, canned goods, and other pantry essentials that do not need to be refrigerated, cooked, or prepared in any other unique way. Many of these foods are undoubtedly already in your pantry. PLEASE TAKE NOTE: You will need to bring along a manual can opener.

Carbohydrates should take up half of your allotment, so you shouldn't forget to include things like rice and pasta. Foods that are high in calories, such as peanut butter, jelly, low-sodium crackers, granola bars, dried fruit, cookies, and hard candies; in addition, remember to include instant coffee and powdered milk. The food should have a protein content of at least 25 percent.

Items that combine dehydrated foods with supplements, such as powdered milk, powdered eggs, dried fruits and vegetables, or cooked dehydrated foods, are good for having a long shelf life while saving space. When there is room, add dried beans; they are more space-efficient than canned beans, but the trade-off is that you have to simmer them in water before eating them.

Add your own sweeteners or substitutions, such as garlic powder, pepper, salt, and sugar. Include any spices that are special to you. Consuming food that lacks flavor can be a source of frustration. Incorporate flavorful meals as well as olive or sunflower oil.

Put the most important cooking implements and utensils in a box with your emergency food supply and keep them there. Check that you have a can opener, some silverware, and a cup with you. A butane or gel stove equipped with a fuel-assist pusher should also be kept on hand.

Additionally, you need to have the following culinary utensils:

A manual can opener.

Eating utensils designed for outdoor use or paper cups and plates wrapped in plastic.

Knives that can be used for a variety of purposes.

Bleach, typically found in households, can be used to purify drinking water.

Aluminum foil and plastic wrap were used.

Plastic shopping bags

A portable stove and a container of fuel are provided for cooking.

You might also refer to it as a "preparation pantry." You should begin by creating a plan for food storage after conducting an inventory of the food that is already present in your home.

The ideal way to store food is in a location that is cool, dark, well-ventilated, and well-organized. The food should be kept in a large container or box that has a date on it that indicates when it will no longer be edible.

You'll need to exercise some ingenuity if you reside in a cramped flat with limited space for food storage. There are a variety of locations in which you are able to store food, including underneath the bed or the sofa in the bedroom, in the closet, covering the boxes with cloth and using them as nightstands or TV tables, using locations above or behind the refrigerator or on top of the washer or dryer, or making use of a garage or a shed (where food is conveniently stored in airtight containers).

The next step would be to estimate the number of guests that will be there as well as the amount of time necessary to stock your pantry.

It is essential to always eat the foods that have the lowest shelf life first and then replace them in order to prevent food from going bad. When deciding what to eat, it is important to take a number of factors into consideration, including how long the meal will last, how it will taste, how much money we have available, how many calories it will contain, and how nutritious it will be. This is because in the event of an emergency, it is most practical to consume the best food that can be obtained. Consider, in a similar vein, the changing of the seasons as well as the lifestyles that we lead.

You should think about the food, but you should also think about the condiments in order to make the cuisine tasty.

How to organize? You don't have to devote an entire day to organizing your "prep pantry." To put it another way, whenever we go shopping, we can always buy some extras and store them away. This will allow us to have our pantry in only a few weeks' time.

Foods That Could Be Prepared If You Think About It Even if you do not have access to gas or electricity.

Maintaining a well-stocked pantry is important to do in the event that there is a disruption in the supply of food.

It is essential to have long-lasting dry meals such as dried, dehydrated, and canned foods that require minimal cooking in case there is a loss of power and that suit both our nutritional and culinary needs. These foods should be stored in a cool, dry place. Consuming foods like fruits and vegetables that have a lengthy shelf life is another option.

You need these things in your vegetables and fruits:

Fresh leafy greens and root vegetables, such as squash, sweet potatoes, or potatoes. They can last for a number of months.

Both fresh garlic and onions have a shelf life of about two months.

Apples have a shelf life of a few weeks at the most.

Dried fruit as a flavoring component for breakfast cereals.

Tomatoes packed in cans

Dried veggies.

Frozen veggies.

Frozen fruit.

Garlic and onion powder respectively.

Seeds that need to be germinated, such as broccoli, alfalfa, spinach, and so on.

For anyone interested in carbs, I suggest:

Oat flakes.

Cotija made from 100% whole wheat.

Bulgur.

Quinoa.

Buckwheat.

Pasta in every conceivable form.

Rice in its purest form

Bread designed to survive a long time, similar to knackebrot.

Alternative flours such buckwheat, oat, spelt, almond, and chickpea flours.

Wraps composed of whole grains

Cereals for breakfast that are sugar-free.

I suggest the following proteins:

Have some dry legumes, including chickpeas, beans, and lentils, for example. They can be of assistance during the germination process.

Various types of canned legumes, include lentils, beans, and others. They can be consumed in their natural state or even used as a spread if there is no light.

Peanut butter, a food that is high in protein.

Legume paste.

Long-lasting tofu.

Chickpea flour. [Note:

A mixture of seed and nut butter.

I would recommend the following condiments:

It is best to keep a wide selection of condiments in the pantry so that they can be used to add flavor to the food in the event of an unexpected circumstance that requires us to cook extremely basic and speedy meals. It's amazing how much of a difference can be made with just a little of spice or some soy sauce.

Olive oil as well as coconut oil.

Apple cider vinegar.

Sea salt.

Pesto.

Mustard.

Soy sauce.

Sweeteners.

Spices.

Cocoa powder.

Vegetable bouillon cubes.

Yeast extract used in nutrition.

Canned vegetable pate.

Flaxseed meal packed in cans.

Baking powder, as well as yeast.

Baking soda for baking desserts.

Powdered milk or veggie drink.

Various infusions, as well as tea and coffee.

Tomatoes that have been dried, capers, and olives.

Milk from canned coconut.

Dried mushrooms.

Don't forget about the superfoods:

Algae that are abundant in certain minerals

Superfoods that are powdered.

The following are some options for snacks:

The finest dark chocolate.

Crackers made with whole grains or oats.

A popcorn of good quality.

Nuts that have not been toasted.

Crunchy kale chips.

Cretons made with cereal

Crisp pieces of baked corn.

Energy bars.

I really hope that you are making a list of everything that you can bring with you so that you can start to establish a survival zone. In the following chapter, I will discuss how to effectively plan and organize food resources.

Chapter 5

HOW TO EFFICIENTLY MANAGE YOUR FOOD SUPPLIES.

I will instruct you on how to preserve food effectively so that you can make the most of the resources available to you. In this way, when a calamity comes, you will have more time to think rationally, with some degree of peace of mind, and you will be able to maximize the use of your resources.

The Most Effective and Secure Methods for Storing Food

It is preferable to have food at home even if you do not require it, rather than to require it and not have it available.

It is my recommendation that you keep the food products that were mentioned above. You don't need to dig a hole in the ground to preserve them if you keep them well-protected and spread them around various places in your home; that's all that's required. You can keep them in different types of locations.

Eat a variety of different kinds of food. To ensure that you can make the most of the potatoes, onions, and other vegetables that you are continuously rotating, keep them all in the same location.

Because you never know where in your home you might be trapped in the event of an emergency, it is best to store your belongings in as many different areas as possible, including the kitchen, the basement, and each and every room in your home.

Maintain an inventory of your storage space. For instance, you purchased a can of food on April 20, 2020, and you notice that it is going to be out of date in 2022. You decide to replace it with another can of food a couple of months before it expires, so that you would always have access to fresh food.

Large plastic baskets can be used to store and arrange food. Inside these containers, you can keep a variety of long-lasting and nourishing foods such as canned fruits and energy bars.

The plan is to arrange these foods in an orderly fashion. In a perfect world, everything would be organized as neatly as it is in your pantry; that way, in the event of a crisis, you would know exactly which foods you had and where they are located.

For instance, in a particular location You can choose from a variety of rice and oatmeal.

Another location is suitable for storing canned foods, candies, and items such as peanut butter or nutella, which are not only delicious but also contain nutrients that, in addition to calories, can be of assistance to you in an emergency situation.

You may also keep food in bottles and cartons, as well as can it and store it, and it will keep for a considerable amount of time. For instance, a bottle made of plastic could be used to store sugar or flour.

Advice on How to Make the Most of the Space You Have for Food Storage

I'm going to demonstrate how you can put food away for at least ten years at a time. Some foods are considered to be non-perishable; but, by storing them in a different container, their shelf life can be extended.

I want to teach you how to build a pantry that will serve your needs for at least ten years.

Get one of those water bottles that holds 5 liters and put the food in it, for example, rice; fill it and put absorbent cotton in it, but make sure it's not too big; soak it in alcohol; light it; and then put it in the container and close it as soon as possible.

You can search the internet for information about the proper way to carry out this task. After that, you place a label on it that describes what it contains and includes the current date.

Put some candle wax that has been melted into the closure for the lid so that the container is entirely sealed. You can get better penetration by applying this with a brush that has been dipped in kerosene. Once more, you can check online to see how this operates.

Keeping Food Hidden From Public View

Before the invention of refrigerators, people in places with colder climates would bury their food in the ground to keep it fresh longer. People in northern Canada, for instance, used to construct storage bins in the permafrost (permafrost on the ground in extremely cold regions) in order to keep their belongings safe. They hid them by burying them in the snow. Unfortunately, many homes have been deprived of them as a result of climate change. Because the levels of permafrost are decreasing slightly every day, the process of preserving summer meat is becoming increasingly difficult.

On the other hand, even though climate change is a concern, researchers are rediscovering the issue of how to store food underground. There are currently developing new options.

When the harvest is at its peak in the late summer, you have the option of canning, drying, or freezing the produce. It is understandable that you would like to get the most out of your summer gardening efforts, but it can be taxing to consume each and every carrot, radish, etc. Sand can also be used as a medium in which to store root vegetables as an alternative method.

What Exactly Is Sand Storage, Anyway?

Did you know that restaurants, grocery stores, and farms in the United States together throw away more food than the average American household does? Sand storage can be a tool for preppers for root vegetable storage.

The idea of storing tubers in addition to other crops like apples has been around for quite some time. Our ancestors or mothers used to store tubers in basements, usually in sand. Using sand helps regulate humidity and keeps vegetables away from excess moisture so they don't rot and extend their shelf life. So how do you store root crops in the sand?

How to Store Root Crops in Sand

Root crops can be stored in sand in two simple ways. First, you can use the vegetable crisper in your fridge as a container. Start with "play" sand, the finely washed sand used to fill the sandbox. Fill the fruit and vegetable bin with a few inches of sand and add root vegetables such as radishes, carrots, beets, or kohlrabi, and any hard-fleshed fruits such as apples or pears. Cover them with sand, leaving a small space between each for air circulation. Fruits should be at least 1 inch apart. Do not wash any produce you store in the sand, as this will accelerate decomposition. Simply brush off the dirt and remove green parts such as carrot or beet tops.

You can also store products on sand in a cardboard or wooden box in a cool basement, storage room, cellar, shed, or even in an unheated garage, as long as the temperature is not below freezing. Simply follow the same procedure as above. Vegetables should be stored separately from apples, which release ethylene gas that accelerates ripening and thus spoil. Tubers that grow vertically, such as carrots and parsnips, can be stored upright in the sand in the same way.

To prolong the life of tubers, it is best to keep them in a dry place for a day or two so that the skin can cure or dry out before burying them in sand.

Potatoes, carrots, radishes, beets, artichokes, onions, leeks, and shallots can be stored in the sand with excellent results. They will keep for up to 6 months. Ginger and cauliflower also store well with sand. Some say that napa cabbage and celery can be stored this way for months.

Why Rotating Food Is Essential for Your Survival

Remember to keep in mind the expiration date of food; almost all of them expire, with the exceptions of:\sHoney.\sSugar.

Salt.

Maple syrup.

Distilled liquors.

Rice in its original form.

Soy sauce.

Pure vanilla extract.

White vinegar.

Corn flour.

Having said that, now I will talk about food rotation and why you must do it.

Use the first-in first-out system. This saves money because you don't waste food. To use the first-in-first-out organization with lists, you should organize your pantry, label foods with expiration dates, and put the oldest foods at the front. Keeping a list of all foods is essential.

In an emergency, you may want to go to the grocery store and buy everything. I do not recommend such an action. The following are some things to take into consideration when designing an emergency storage room or pantry:

Products absolutely necessary for your pantry. The cost of food is not zero. It is more important to make smart purchases than it is to spend a lot of money on a large quantity of food.

Threats to the safety of stored food. The ability to store food is affected by factors such as temperature, oxygen, light, weather, insects, and humidity.

Date of expiration and rotation of food supplies. You should keep a record of the length of time that each food item can be stored, and you should rotate older items before purchasing replacements.

Diets for diabetics or other special diets are an additional concern regarding food (low carbohydrate, low fat, low salt, or other products). The shelf life of certain dehydrated foods can range anywhere from 20 to 30 years.

Almost all preppers make several food storage mistakes. It is difficult to resist. Even the most seasoned survivalists are prone to making mistakes every once in a while. Because of this, I believed that the second part of the section that dealt with common errors in food storage would serve as a useful reminder.

Having the intention to stockpile, but never actually doing so: Planning something can often feel like an accomplishment in and of itself, but if you never move beyond the planning stage, you are wasting your time and effort.

Purchasing the food and then failing to remember where it is: It does not necessarily mean that you are prepared simply because you have purchased a large quantity of food and stashed it away in the pantry.

Purchasing in large quantities of foods that you have never tasted before: What if all of those Alfredo boxes of freeze-dried chicken were a complete and utter disappointment? Do you not believe that it is in your best interest to find out before you are compelled to consume it on a daily basis? If you ask, most companies that sell food storage products will send you a sample of their product.

purchasing in large quantities solely due to the fact that there was a discount: If you do not enjoy the food, this is not a good deal for you. Do not give in to the temptation of purchasing food simply because it is currently on sale.

You and your loved ones will have a much easier time recovering from a calamity if you are able to maintain your normal eating routine after the event. There is an old proverb that goes, "Eat to save, save to eat."

Forgetting about variety: If you want to avoid hearing complaints from family members like "Beans again?," don't buy too much of just one item.

Food fatigue is a very real phenomenon, and research has shown that eating something new for dinner each night can help improve one's mood.

Investing in a lot of perishable food that needs to be stored in the refrigerator: I'm all for stocking refrigerators, but if the power is out for more than a few days, you're going to need to find some other solutions.

Storing foods that are difficult to prepare is a questionable mistake due to the fact that some people are excellent cooks even when they do not have access to electricity. However, the majority of people should select foods that do not require a great deal of preparation time. You should try to make use of as few resources as is humanly possible.

Not taking into account the various seasonings and spices: It is simple to forget about them, but it is imperative that you do not. Without them, certain foods would have almost no flavor or interest to eat at all.

Forgetting to label food and indicate the expiration date: If you don't know how long the food has been sitting around, you'll either have to throw it away or run the risk of consuming something that will make you sick. Acquire the ability to read the expiration dates on food.

Using food storage containers that aren't very durable: Avoid putting food in cardboard boxes at all costs. Put them in a location that is inaccessible to insects and other vermin. You might want to try putting food in a Mylar bag.

Keeping food in places that are high in humidity and have a fluctuating temperature: Locate a spot in your house that maintains a consistent temperature and level of humidity. Think about different locations where you could keep food.

Ignoring the practice of food rotation: If you don't want everything to go bad, you should establish a reliable system for rotating the food.

Leaving off an itemized list of the inventory: This will assist you in determining what to purchase next and will prevent you from purchasing food that you already have. It would be best if you could avoid doing it on a computer. After the disaster, you do not know if you will have access to electricity; therefore, it is best to err on the side of caution and use pen and paper.

Equipment for the preparation of food that was not present: The first item on the list is a tool for opening cans. In addition to that, you might require a hand mixer, a grinder (if you have wheat), a camp stove, and various other non-electric home appliances.

Tips for Keeping Your Pet's Supplies in Order

I want to show you how to put away food for your animals in a location where you will need it in order to ensure your own survival in the event of a disaster. If you have a pet at home, one of your primary concerns is likely to be ensuring that they are healthy and have access to the food they require.

Remember to figure out how much food your pet consumes every month and then multiply that number so that there is enough food for many months, if not years, to come.

You can purchase a large container made of plastic that has a flip-top lid and a gasket around it. This will not only keep the food dry and fresh, but it will also protect it from bugs that want to eat it.

If you don't have enough food on hand, you can also store the food for your dog and cat in a bucket that has a capacity of 5 gallons.

Be sure to switch up the order in which you feed your pet's food so that the shelf life can be extended as much as possible.

If you have the lid that snaps on, you can use the absorbent cotton method to close it, which will allow you to get more use out of it and will also extend its lifespan.

In the same way that you would prepare for a family member's unique requirements, you should gather all of the essential items for your pet into one container and store it in the bunker. This should include all necessary documentation as well as food, water, and other necessities. The following items should be included in this package:

You are required to have medications, medical records, and proof of vaccinations, particularly the rabies vaccine, and you must store them in a container that is waterproof.

Carrying case, shoulder straps, and safety belts are included.

Should your pet require one, a muzzle (e.g., for a dog).

Food and water, as well as a manual can opener should be brought.

In the event that you need to evacuate, make sure to bring your cat's litter box with you.

In the event that you lose your pet, bring a recent photo of it along with a description of it.

Your veterinarian's full name, as well as their address and phone number.

Please provide the appropriate contact information for the insurance company if you have a pet policy.

If you must leave your home, take your pets with you.

Be ready to leave as soon as possible; do not wait for the police to come and ask you to leave; in this situation, it may not be permitted to bring your pets with you.

At all times, keep your pet in a carrier cratc or on a leash.

Ensure that your pet's identification tag is current and that it is always worn. If you lose your pet or become lost, it can be helpful to have a friend's or family member's phone number on a tag or in your database so you can reach them even if you are not at home in your neighborhood.

Following the Tragedy

Keep your pet from running when you get home. Though it's simple to get lost in these circumstances, familiar sights and smells can aid him in orienting himself.

Do not rush. Work to return your pet to a normal life as soon as you can, and keep an eye out for strange attitudes and behaviors that may be signs of stress. Call your veterinarian if these symptoms don't improve after a few days and keep an eye out for any changes in your pet's routine.

Don't let your pets play in water-filled areas because these features can conceal dangers like canals and wells, venomous animals like snakes and lizards, and even live wires, increasing the risk of electrocution.

Then, in the final chapter, I'll demonstrate how to store food for a long time and have a variety of foods in your bunker.

Chapter 6

lists twelve different methods for keeping food fresh.

Food can be preserved in a variety of ways to prolong its shelf life. Additionally to adding variety to the bunker beyond flour and canned goods, you will have preserved containers that will last for a very long time. If you make them as I instruct here, you will be able to stay composed and concentrate on your family during a crisis.

Always be careful when measuring, which means to figure out how many people will eat the food so that you have the appropriate portions for the duration of the meal.

Canning in a Water Bath

A thermal process called a "water bath," which involves heating food in boiling water, is used to can high-acid, acidified, or high-sugar foods at home.

When properly applied, this technique, which revolves boiling water around the canning jar, can eradicate microorganisms that thrive on foods with a pH below 4.6, such as most fruits, tomatoes, and pickles, as well as foods with high sugar contents (above 65° brix), such as jams, jellies, and syrups.

In order to sterilize canned foods in a water bath, the food must first be sealed in glass jars and then exposed to boiling water for a sufficient amount of time to kill any microbes that may already be present. There are two stages to the process: heating and cooling.

The food's volume increases as it heats, and the air is forced out of the container. This stage involves the removal of microorganisms and a few enzymatic reactions that ensure the quality of the upcoming preserves.

The preserves slowly return to room temperature and their original volume during the cooling process. A vacuum is produced, sealing the lid because there is no air in the upper space. By keeping air from returning to the product, this vacuum seal prevents recontamination.

Knowing specific feeding, packaging, and heating treatment parameters is necessary before beginning to make homemade bain-marie preserves in order to get better results.

Choosing and handling food products properly

The bain-marie method should only be used to preserve extremely acidic or acidified foods with a pH below 4.6, such as pickles, jams, jellies, and syrups, it should be emphasized again.

When fresh foods are at their ripest, choose them.

Choose fruits of comparable size that are lump- and bruise-free when canning whole fruits.

Foods need to be washed thoroughly, handled as quickly as possible, and handled hygienically. They should never be exposed to room temperature unnecessarily, and if an unexpected event prevents the preparation from continuing, they should be refrigerated until it does.

Bain-Marie preserves-compatible containers

Homemade preserves should be stored in glass jars that are specifically made for this use, preferably with a wide mouth. On the market, there are many varieties, and you can even use the jars from other preserves. Jars with nicks, cracks, and jagged edges should be inspected, and those that cannot seal or crack during heat treatment should be discarded.

Check the gaskets or rubbers on the caps, and make sure the threaded strips are not dented or corroded, if the caps are not brand-new. Replace any metal caps that have inner lacquer layers that are worn or damaged if you plan to use metal caps; the lacquer is necessary to shield the caps from AHA.

If the preserves are heat-treated for longer than 10 minutes, the water bath will sterilize both the jar and its contents. Otherwise, wash the jars and lids thoroughly and sterilize them after cleaning.

Although they cannot guarantee a vacuum seal and are relatively expensive, jars with glass lids and latex gaskets are very decorative. Whenever they are repeatedly exposed to boiling water, their closed system or metal clips tend to rust.

Screw-top jars with a tight button are the best containers by a long shot for bain-marie preserves. In contrast to the airtight cap, which can only be used once, the screw cap can be used repeatedly.

Jars with metal screw caps are a good option because they are simple to find and affordable. If the protective paint is still intact and the label is closed, metal stoppers can be reused; however, it is always advised to buy new stoppers.

Is this a secure technique? Yes, provided that the correct procedures are followed for cleaning the jars, lids, and food preparation. The boiling time must be observed, which is most important. With this method, extreme caution must be exercised because improperly prepared preserves run the risk of being contaminated with botulinum toxin, which can lead to botulism, a condition that can be fatal in 5–10% of cases. Preparations with a high sugar content or acidic preserves (tomato, lemon, or vinegar) cannot produce this toxin.

Foods that can be preserved in a water bath include what? Jams, syrups, brines, meats, fish, vegetables, mushrooms, fruits, and cooked foods (pasta, beans, soups, stews, creams).

Pressurized Canning

Instead of making their own food preserves, younger generations are accustomed to purchasing jars and cans of food from a grocery store.

However, a lot of people still are aware of this old and fundamental technique's secrets. For when disaster strikes and we need food, demand has prompted people to develop techniques like these.

For this reason, I want to provide a comprehensive breakdown of the entire procedure as a small general guide for making preserves at home, with special attention to the sterilization of the container and the gradual elimination of the filling.

The ingredients must first be carefully chosen to be as fresh and complete as possible. Try to select pieces of produce that are similar in size and at the ideal point of ripeness for both fruits and vegetables.

Most of the time, raw materials need to be pre-treated before packaging.

To make jam or syrup, for instance, fruit needs to be washed, peeled, and cut before being cooked with sugar, citric acid, and pectin. Sterilization is advised because the high sugar concentrations produce an anaerobic environment that limits the growth of some but not all bacteria. Before being preserved, vegetables can go through a number of different processes. So, green beans or artichokes are blanched or cooked first, followed by the roasting of peppers, the cooking of tomatoes, and possibly the crushing and reduction of tomatoes. The new method of cooking has issues if you don't add enough acidity to the food; it must be done in the pot instead. Pickles typically don't require pre-heating before serving.

Although it can also be simply marinated and served, soaking in oil, pickles, etc., if you want to make canned fish, such as tuna, mackerel, or anchovies, the previous process is usually a longer heat treatment, such as peeling and boning the food and then boiling or roasting it.

It's crucial to take the pH level of the food product into account when canning it. The pH scale is used to assess acidity. Foods that have a pH below 4.5 are regarded as acidic, but canning is not a significant issue.

It might be necessary to add an acidity regulator to canned foods if they contain low-acid foods with a pH of greater than 4.5, such as meat, fish, or the majority of canned vegetables and fruits. By stabilizing the pH, these correction additives stop the growth of harmful bacteria and microorganisms in the medium.

Use a pH meter or pH tape with color-banded acidity classification to determine a product's alkalinity. To measure the pH of the sample, a simple instrument with a sensor is inserted into the food and called a pH meter.

Each food's pH is not constant; it varies with respect to the food's maturity, origin, variety, and even temperature (so it is advisable to measure at room temperature).

However, it's simple to find tables on the Internet that approximate how acidic most foods are, especially fruits and vegetables. These tables can be used as a guide and don't necessarily require strict controls.

As I've already stated, in order to sterilize and package low-acid foods for storage, it is frequently necessary to attempt to make up for their lack of acidity through a procedure known as acidification.

Typically, vinegar, citric acid, or ascorbic acid is added to the preserving liquid to opacify vegetables that have been blanched to preserve their properties before being used to make homemade preserves (usually water and salt). These ingredients not only change the pH but also function as antioxidants.

The issue is that while this conditioning liquid can occasionally flavor and enhance the flavor of aromatic plants and spices, in this instance the necessary acidification can slightly detract from the final product's flavor. Whatever the case, acidification alone is not a method of preservation; rather, it is a step that must be taken to preserve some foods prior to autoclaving.

As a natural preservative, oil, on the other hand, can be used to increase the shelf life of precooked foods or vegetables like peppers or sundried tomatoes.

Our peppers are preserved by the oil added to the juices released by the peppers themselves during roasting, rather than the product being ruined by adding a lot of vinegar or other correcting acids.

Making Vegetable Preserves at Home

Veggies that have been cooked or blanched (high pH): After the required blanching, sterilize the jars in addition to adding an acidity corrector to the mulching liquid; otherwise, sterilize in a pressure cooker. When there is no other DIY method to keep vegetables airtight and the acidification and overcooking are bad for them, the best choice is usually to blanch and freeze them.

Fish that has been home-canned as well as prepared foods (which can be preserved in oil): Fill the jars with oil and sterilize them by cooking them for a long time in a bain-marie after preparing and cooking the food. Anchovies, which are regarded as semi-canned because they have not been heated, should be kept in the refrigerator.

Making Syrup-Based Homemade Fruit Preserves

Fruit in syrup needs to be peeled, cut, washed, and kept until it is packed at the proper stage of ripeness in brine and lemon juice. Place the fruit in a jar, then top with the extremely hot syrup and simmer for 30 minutes.

Making Homemade Jam and Preserves

Making the jam Add sugar, pectin, and citric acid (as appropriate for the pH of each fruit) (the natural component of the fruit that gives it a sticky consistency). Powdered pectin needs to be added in a specific quantity because the amount of natural pectin varies greatly depending on the type of fruit. Each jar contains hot jam that is either sterilized in a bain-marie or not sterilized at all to preserve it (if the amount of sugar is so high that the sugar acts as a preservative and ensures preservation). Chutney is a unique instance where sugar and acid combine to preserve the product.

Fermentation

In the absence of oxygen, nutrients are fermented to produce energy. In other words, bacteria that carry out specific tasks in our bodies—tasks without which we cannot survive—are created by the biochemical process of converting one organic material into another.

But what advantages do eating foods that have undergone fermentation while you are protected offer?

They also give you the following advantages:

They aid in pre-digesting food and replenishing the flora in your intestinal tract.

Food now has better nutrition because it doesn't lose its properties; on the contrary, it gains them.

They perform a number of tasks including digestion, nutrient absorption, vitamin synthesis, and transporter regulation. They also have probiotic properties.

They are a time-honored, reliable, and secure method of food preservation.

I'll demonstrate this with some cabbage sauce:

You'll need it if:

Cabbage\sSalt

Mode of preparation:

Spices and dried fruits are required (pepper, cumin, fennel, chili, sunflower or pumpkin seeds, cranberries, raisins, fennel...).

To keep the air out, you need an airtight jar.

The cabbage needs to be chopped or shredded first.

To remove the moisture, add salt to the chopped vegetables in a sizable bowl (not plastic) and mash by hand.

Add your preferred spices, dried fruit, or nuts to the mixture once you notice that they have released enough water.

Vegetables can be tightly packed so that they are compelled to stay below the liquid. After pressing, cover with a leaf and cap the jar.

The fermenters are now in your possession, and they will be edible in 4 to 6 weeks.

Dehydration and Drying

Food dehydration entails taking out the majority of the water present in a food in order to achieve low water activity and halt microbial growth.

We will use the terms dehydrated and dried interchangeably here unless it is necessary to differentiate because that is not technically accurate to describe the moisture condition of foods after they have undergone the drying process. A dried food is one that has a moisture content above 2.5 percent as opposed to a dehydrated product, which has a moisture content below 2.5 percent.

Food drying is suitable for fruits, vegetables, herbs, mushrooms, fish, meat, and many prepared foods. It also has a wide range of uses.

I'll Show You How to Use Solar Energy.

You can dry things directly. The product to be dried is placed directly on a table or rack in the sun; the sun's rays and the wind remove the moisture from the food. This is the simplest and most traditional method of dehydration.

sun-powered dehydrator Devices that use solar energy to dry food either directly or indirectly come in a wide variety of types and specifications. It consists of a chamber where the food is arranged on a grid and hot air is circulated through it, gradually removing the humidity.

drying in a solar oven. Dehydrating food is one of the most intriguing uses for a solar oven; by making a few adjustments to its usual operating mode, it can effectively serve as a solar dehydrator. You can use the solar oven at any time of the year to dehydrate fruits and other foods without wasting electricity. Since the product is not exposed to weather conditions or the whims of birds and insects, it dries much more quickly than direct sunlight and is hygienic.

Dehydrated foods generally have a number of benefits, including:

Due to the low loss of vitamins compared to other preservation techniques, they have a high nutritional value.

enables you to safely store almost any kind of food, regardless of how acidic it is.

It is not necessary to add preservatives.

Natural sugars are concentrated when water is partially removed, giving dried foods a richer flavor.

Foods that have been dehydrated are simple to store and don't require special packaging, freezing, or cooling. They also take up very little space due to their small size.

They can be consumed in many different ways, including as dried fruit or as an ingredient in recipes.

Food that has been dried is nutritious and light, making it the perfect choice for outdoor activities like hiking.

However, there are additional advantages to dehydrating food and fruit at home.

By selecting your food, you can be sure of its provenance and that it meets your standards for the best quality.

When you dehydrate food at home, you can see exactly when it was made and packaged. Additionally, your products won't be exposed to the elements or contamination in the market or store in terms of hygiene and handling conditions.

By making your own dehydrated foods, you can create unique, personalized products that are either hard to find or not available on the market, allowing you to create delicious snacks and vegetable appetizers as well as use them as ingredients in baking recipes.

They enable you to take advantage of inexpensive seasonal foods that can be preserved for later consumption and boost the household economy. Dehydrating food is a very practical way to stop freshly harvested food from going bad if we have a vegetable garden.

How to Dehydrate Foods, Including Fruits

No matter the method used to dehydrate food, the right conditions must be in place to guarantee a steady flow of hot air that is low in moisture and the right temperature.

Each food has unique properties and consequently needs to be dried according to those characteristics. Don't forget that food can also be preserved by dehydrating it. Since you won't be following any instructions when you prepare the food, it's critical that you do so correctly.

To dehydrate food, generally speaking, the following procedures should be followed:

Foods that have been dried should be kept in an airtight container that is labeled with the date of preparation.

Products should be carefully washed before dehydrating, and any that are damaged or overripe should be thrown away. Then, the food's unusable components, including the skin, roots, and stems, as well as any rotten or immature components, should be eliminated.

Depending on the food and the desired final appearance, cut into cubes, blocks, slices, or strips that are between 0.5 and 1 cm thick to encourage dehydration.

Foods should frequently be processed before drying to prevent color or texture changes that could degrade the final product's appearance or quality.

Foods that have been properly prepared and placed in the dehydrator should be distributed evenly on the tray to enable uniform drying.

Those pieces that weren't properly dried or those that displayed any abnormalities should be separated after the dehydration process is complete.

To prevent the reabsorption of moisture from the environment, dehydrated foods should be packed as soon as possible. Packaging needs to be done in polypropylene bags or airtight containers. Each container should be marked with the date of manufacture, and it should be kept in a cool, dark location.

All foods are not dried in the same way, even though the drying process generally follows the general steps above. Depending on the food type, different temperatures are advised for dehydration, and some products allow you to use higher temperatures than others. On the other hand, some foods need to be pre-treated before they can be dehydrated in order to enhance the final product's texture, flavor, or color or to make the moisture removal process easier.

Knowing how to properly evaluate the end of the process is another crucial element when dehydrating food; incomplete or partial drying can result in the product spoiling after temporary storage. On the other hand, excessive dehydration can lead to a product with a poor texture and quality. The technique for assessing sweetness differs depending on the particular food.

Pasteurization

Before consumption, raw juices, cider, and milk should all be pasteurized. If handled correctly, it can eliminate almost all harmful bacteria that are present in these fluids. Although heating liquids directly is a good option, the water bath is likely the best at-home method.

the following steps:

In a big pot, put your storage container. Put the container and lid inside it with care. They ought to hold still and avoid running into one another.

Boiling water Set the pot over a stovetop with high heat. Once the water has reached a rolling boil, submerge the container and its lid for a minimum of ten minutes.

Take out and dry. Remove the container and lid with care from the hot water after turning off the heat. They should be spread out on a clean, dry kitchen towel to drain outside.

Get a bain-marie pot ready. Water should be added to the lower bowl of the double boiler to a height of about 5 cm (2 inches). Insert the first part inside the smaller upper part.

Incorporate smaller containers with the liquid. Fill the smaller container in the water bath with the liquid that needs to be pasteurized.

On the stove, warm a pan for a water bath. Place the entire pot on the stove and warm it over a medium-high flame.

You have to keep things at the right temperature. The pasteurized liquids should be allowed to reach 72 °C (162 °F). Remove the lid of the bain-marie pot from the heat after maintaining it at this temperature for longer than 16 seconds.

the liquid into a container that has been sterilized. Carefully pour it into a previously sterilized container after removing it from the heat.

Quickly cool them. Give the container 15 minutes to stand in cold water after it has been filled.

The method to wash it is as follows:

one substantial sink

It is not necessary for the water to be ice cold, but it should be considerably colder than room temperature. Do not put the jar in the fridge or freezer as soon as you bring it inside because it may crack from the extreme cold.

Keep things cool when storing. Put the jars in the refrigerator after quickly cooling them in water.

Within six hours, the liquid ought to reach a temperature of less than 4°C (40°F).

Even after the initial cooling process, you should keep it in the refrigerator. Pasteurized milk keeps for up to two weeks, but juice and cider keep for four.

Griddling Meat

The process of smoking meat involves cooking it until it is completely dry. It becomes very tender as a result of the process, which gradually breaks down the fat and connective tissue. Selecting meat that tastes good and has a smoky flavor is crucial. In the wild, smoking fish, reptiles, and large mammals is a common practice.

Trim the available meat, removing any excess skin, fat, and bones. Trimming is necessary because fat will ruin the meat and the cut. The meat should be cut into 1/4-inch-thick strips. On the meat's surface, sprinkle some salt.

Continue by removing the meat's moisture.

To prepare the meat strips for this step, you should attach them to a stick and set them about two feet above a bed of hot coals. Don't let the meat sit out for too long, though, as you are only removing the moisture, not cooking, it. Meat that has been dehydrated resists spoilage, and heat destroys any bacteria it may contain.

The Method of Smoking

You may now start smoking! The right wood can help you achieve your goal of not smothering the fire with excessive smoke. Insects like flies are prevented from laying eggs on the meat by a film that is produced on it by both the smoke and the heat.

Be patient and assured.

The smoker's temperature affects how long bacon takes to cook. Bacon typically cooks for 6 to 8 hours. The best way to know when the procedure is complete is through touch. Frequently check to see if it is dry. It is sufficiently dry if the meat splits.

I advise you to cook the meat before eating it so that bacteria are eliminated for your safety. Additionally, bear in mind that while smoking can extend the life of the meat, it must be stored properly. Keep in mind that leftover bacon won't be edible indefinitely and has a high likelihood of spoiling due to bacterial buildup since it is unlikely that you will have a refrigerator in the wild.

Salting

Because it is necessary for cooking, salt is a necessary ingredient in every home. It is only applied as flavoring in the food industry to improve the flavors of other ingredients, such as binders and dehydrating agents. The ability to preserve food is a very significant additional use of salt.

Although it is a common practice, adding salt to food is mostly associated with food that is ready to eat because of the flavor it imparts, which is a favorite of many people. This is true for all foods, not just salty ones. For example, chocolate-based sweets can benefit from a dash of salt.

In the process of food preservation, salt is added to food to stop the growth of bacteria and mold, extending the amount of time that food can be consumed without endangering one's health.

Pickling or salting of food is the name for this salt preservation technique. Despite the fact that this method is typically used for marinating fish and meat, it can also be used to prepare fruits and vegetables.

I'll use fish as an example to explain it to you, but the concept is applicable to other foods as well.

Five steps make up the most typical fish salting procedure:

Washing: Before beginning, wash the fish to get rid of the guts and prepare it for the process.

Stacking: As a bed on which to place the fish, add a layer of salt one centimeter thick to a container or surface. On top of this layer of fish, add a layer of salt with a similar thickness. Repeat, alternating between layers of fish and salt. Place a weight on top of the fish stack that is at least half its weight. A uniform salt distribution throughout each layer must be made during this step.

Time spent relaxing: Depending on the marinade, this step may change. While the previous stack can be allowed to rest for up to 24 hours, the typical rest period is one and a half weeks.

Cleaning: Take the fish out from between the salt layers after the allotted resting period and wash it in a water and vinegar solution.

Drying: After the fish has finished marinating, it should be dried in a semi-controlled environment with airflow but moderate sunlight exposure.

The product can be kept in the container for a very long time after the marinating process is complete. Nuts can be added to it before serving, or it can be re-seasoned with salt and seasoning spices like paprika, cinnamon, dill seeds, etc.

Alcohol Submersion

Since the Roman era, the Gauls have been familiar with alcohol. Alchemy, however, and the terms alcohol and distiller are Arab in origin. In the peninsula, the Arabs introduced distillation methods. Since its inception, people have been aware of alcohol's miraculous qualities and therapeutic uses. It is also flavored with fruits and plants to improve its medicinal properties.

Steps to take:

The secret recipe for many elixirs and liqueurs, which has been passed down from generation to generation, involves steeping fruits and plants in wine. However, a new phase in the development of liqueurs began in the 18th century with the introduction of sugar and spices from the West Indies.

The best-known preservative is alcohol. Numerous fruits and vegetables can be soaked in it, and it can also be used to dilute sugar to taste and lower the alcohol content by adding distilled water.

Fruits are macerated with alcohol during a process called maceration, but the alcohol also imparts flavor and aroma to the fruit mixture. It is best to use white wine alcohol or wine alcohol with specific nuances, aromas, and flavors, like Brandy or Cognac, when making homemade preservatives.

Alcohol is very effective at perfectly preserving some fruits, but only if it contains a high amount of alcohol because the water from the fruit plant mixes with the alcohol and lowers its alcohol content. In order to prevent distorting the fruit's flavor, it should also be flavorless. Consequently, depending on the kind of fruit being processed, it is best to use living water at 50 to 70° (122-158°F).

Alcohol should not be used to preserve fruits that are not fully ripe, healthy, and very fresh, free of cracks, cuts, or bruises, and without insect bites. Because of their delicate skins, peaches should be peeled, and stone fruits should be pricked several times to keep them from splitting and letting alcohol inside.

Let the fruit soak in alcohol for about a month and a half before adding more or less sugar, depending on how the fruit has been processed. It tastes delicious to eat citrus fruits in cans that have been soaked and preserved with heat-resistant pomace in a porcelain dish.

Oil or fat preservation

One method of food preservation used since the dawn of time is the use of a fatty medium. It entails completely covering the food in fat, which can be lard or extra virgin olive oil. Food is longer-preserved as a result of avoiding contact with air.

I'll use cheese as an example and give it to you.

When cheese is specially preserved with extra virgin olive oil, it not only extends the preservation period but also prevents the cheese from becoming overly hard, which improves the flavor of the cheese.

how to use aromatic oils for cheese preservation.

By incorporating spices into the oil, you can also give the cheese new flavors.

The steps are easy to follow:

Cheese should be rind-free.

Make small cuts.

The flavorings you select should be placed in a glass jar with a hermetic seal.

Until everything is covered, add extra virgin olive oil.

Put the lid on the jar and store it somewhere cool and dry. You can use it after two weeks.

Thyme and rosemary are favorites of goat cheese. Truffle flavoring makes cow cheese even more delectable; we can either add truffle to the oil or add a small amount of truffle oil. The spicy taste is ideal for this kind of cheese.

Freezing

I want to discuss organizing this area and how to keep food chilled in your bunker. Utilize plastic bags in the freezer to create an established system and make use of the available space.

Sausage, blueberries, and other items can be placed in this area to be chilled. When you get home from the grocery store, swap out any frozen food, such as sausages, for the food that is in the refrigerator so that you can easily rotate it in case of emergency.

Fruits and vegetables in the freezer

If they are homemade, store them in a freezer bag that is clipped shut or in plastic wrap and mark the date on the bag or wrap. Fruit that has been home-frozen can last for eight months to a year.

Products Made from Bread

For up to three months, store them collectively.

Leftovers

Put them in freezer-safe containers just like your homemade purees and soups. Put dates on them. Foods containing cooked meat or poultry will remain fresh for two to six months. Place meals prepared at home in oven-safe containers and wrap in aluminum foil. By doing this, you can reheat them straight from the refrigerator. They can last for four to six months.

Since it can be challenging to separate units that are frozen together, divide foods like sausage into individual portions and store them in plastic bags with seals and labels. Sausage and bacon should keep for a month or two.

You can keep chicken or turkey in the freezer for up to a year. Raw meats should be kept on the bottom shelf to prevent any liquid from dripping onto other foods. Fresh meat can be preserved for up to a year, depending on the kind and cut.

Fish

Take a look at the package's expiration date. Fresh fish can be kept for up to 4 months in the case of oily fish and up to 10 months in the case of white fish.

Freeze-Drying

A food preservation technique called freeze-drying relies on the sublimation of water present in certain materials to dry them out. The process involves freezing the product, removing the ice with sublimation, and then heating it while under vacuum.

Strawberry freeze-dried snacks are a tasty and wholesome treat. To keep the food from spoiling and to lower its weight, the moisture is taken out of it during the freeze-drying procedure. You can perform it in your home oven or freeze dryer.

I'd like to demonstrate to you how to make dried strawberries.

Strawberries that have been dehydrated can be consumed immediately, added to dishes, or vacuum sealed to preserve them.

Use cold water to rinse strawberries. For the best flavor and texture, use fresh strawberries. Sprinkle strawberries with tap water, then rinse them for 30 to 60 seconds under cold water.

Use a fresh towel to pat the strawberries dry. They shouldn't be overly wet when you start the process. To get rid of the surplus moisture, dry them with a cloth or paper towel. It is important to consider their exterior, especially if it is dry to the touch.

Utilizing a sharp knife, trim the stems. The strawberry stems should be cut with a knife. Since these stems cannot be consumed, they need not be used in the drying process.

Strawberries should be sliced with a thickness of no more than 6 millimeters (24 mm). Cut the strawberries vertically into small pieces using a small to medium knife. To ensure even drying, keep the slices at a thickness of about 1/4" (6 mm).

For proper use of the freeze dryer, read the instructions. A freeze dryer is a machine that automatically freezes food at a low temperature first, then removes all of the moisture. You should read the device's instructions before using a freeze dryer because each one is a little bit different.

Use freezer or parchment paper to line a tray. Trays are included with freeze dryers so that food can be held there while drying. The parchment or freezer paper should be laid on top after being cut to fit the pan.

On the tray, spread them out evenly. The strawberries should not overlap as you place the parchment on the tray. For best results, allow a small gap between each.

Then, put the insulating cover back on the tray and place it in the freeze dryer. The strawberries are prepared for freeze-drying once the tray is full. Place the tray in the proper slot, then lock the machine. To replace the exterior insulating cover, turn it in a clockwise direction.

After you've locked the door, click "Start". Secure it by closing it and turning the handle. When you have finished, look for a sizable "Go" button at the top. When you press it, the device turns on and begins to dry your clothes.

The following day, inspect the strawberries. In about 24 hours, they will be fully dry. The machine will dry the strawberries for an additional 12 hours after freezing them for about 9 hours. Once the drying cycle is complete, turn the machine on and give it a taste.

When the strawberries are fully dried, thaw the machine. The machine will automatically enter the "defrost" mode once you remove the items. This takes place as soon as the freeze dryer clears out the remaining ice and thaws back to room temperature. Once finished, the procedure takes about 2 hours, and the machine is then ready for use once more.

Picking

The best way to ensure that your food is properly preserved, regardless of the method you choose from those mentioned in this chapter, is to choose high-quality ingredients. Avoid using products that have already been abused or that aren't very ripe because it makes no sense to store foods that aren't of high enough quality to eat fresh.

According to what the family members or those who will be in the bunker like, the choice is crucial, as I previously stated.

The idea is that even though you have to be locked up here, you'll have good food and live as comfortably as you can under the circumstances.

CONCLUSION

Natural disasters are happening more frequently as the planet changes. There are increasingly spectacular and unexpected catastrophes as a result of the changing climate, and people's faith in the ability of institutions to deal with disasters is eroding.

It was more or less obvious with the 2020 pandemic that medical institutions in the

United States and other countries cannot sustain a humanitarian disaster; even though they managed to survive, they were under pressure.

In the most recent pandemic years, supply chains struggled. We must devise our own means of sustaining ourselves until the world stabilizes because if the unavoidable occurs—a nuclear war or something else when civilians are unsure how to respond—it will be difficult to maintain production.

Many people are prepared to tackle these issues calmly because we have already set up our lives to be ready for them.

The term "preppers" was once hardly ever searched online, but in recent years, usage has increased significantly. There are also numerous communities on websites like Reddit that discuss preppers in great detail.

It's never too early to start; in fact, you need to get started as quickly as you can. People consider having this plan on hand whenever there is a storm, tsunami, earthquake, or, more lately, a virus. I have, in fact, been preparing for years.

Ready to become a prepper? To give your family the best chance of surviving a catastrophic catastrophe, the question is whether you are ready to be prepared when or if it occurs.

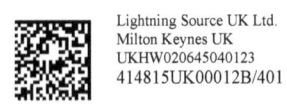

Lightning Source UK Ltd.
Milton Keynes UK
UKHW020645040123
414815UK00012B/401